Splash

A journey through living words

GEORGE THOMAS

BLUEROSE PUBLISHERS
India | U.K.

Copyright © George Thomas 2023

All rights reserved by author. No part of this publication may be reproduced, stored in a retrieval system or transmitted in any form or by any means, electronic, mechanical, photocopying, recording or otherwise, without the prior permission of the author. Although every precaution has been taken to verify the accuracy of the information contained herein, the publisher assume no responsibility for any errors or omissions. No liability is assumed for damages that may result from the use of information contained within.

BlueRose Publishers takes no responsibility for any damages, losses, or liabilities that may arise from the use or misuse of the information, products, or services provided in this publication.

For permissions requests or inquiries regarding this publication, please contact:

BLUEROSE PUBLISHERS
www.BlueRoseONE.com
info@bluerosepublishers.com
+91 8882 898 898
+4407342408967

ISBN: 978-93-5819-643-6

Cover design: Tahira
Typesetting: Tanya Raj Upadhyay

First Edition: October 2023

Preface

Welcome to the world of "Splash,"

This book is a reflection of the human experience—of love, loss, joy, heartache, hope, and everything in between.

"Splash" offers a sanctuary where emotions are celebrated, embraced, and given voice...encouraging you to embrace the madness of emotions that shape your being.

Table of Contents

The devil's bride 1

Perfectly flawed. 3

She 5

Shameless 7

I too have loved 9

I am the fallen one, to this angel. 11

Broken arrows.. 13

Angel wings. 15

Loving to a fault 17

Magnetic persona. 19

Strangers in a bed 21

The best feeling than a high. 23

Years in those eyes 25

Wildfire. 27

Whispers of love 29

My forbidden fruit 31

Pen pal. 33

Kill me softly! 35

Sad girls and bad boys. 37

Rose tinted eyes. 39

Used to use you.	41
When forever isn't long enough.	43
Mysterious ways	45
With you, my world revolves.	47
Presence of you.	49
Knocking at your door	51
An ode to love	53
A million to one shot.	55
Ghosts of the past	57
Yet her	59
False hopes	61
Everything love n other intoxicants	63
Au revoir my love.	65
Forever Bloom.	66
My immoral whispers.	68
Pixie dust	70
Rolling stone.	72
My solace	74
Screw me holier.	76
Shooting star	78
Without rose tinted glasses.	80
With You	82
My silver lining on cloud nine.	84

Surrealistic love	86
Under these quilts	88
You're my missing puzzle pieces.	90
Let me be your last mistake	92
Schizophrenic	94
Queen of Misery	96
My unseen friend named God.	98

The devil's bride

She is a million thoughts in other eyes,
The one that sets everyone's heart raise.
Her ways define who she is.
The light that brightens even the oceans.

Her beauty leaves you mesmerized.
The touch that leaves you paralyzed.
Under her shade, you walk,
In her footsteps, you get lost.

She is a force to be reckoned with,
She is the frosting in everyone's cake,
The cherry on top.
The music to your heart.

Luxury, sin and the city.
She is the type that leaves you grieving,
For more of her
For you know, where you belong.

She brings life to nothingness,
Meaning to your emptiness
She'll make your darkest desires scream.
Making you wish to make your heart stop pounding.

She is the one whom dreams follow
The one whom you beg for forgiveness
The woman you fall for again and again,
But you will never love again.

Perfectly flawed.

Time has never been an essence, so I let it slip.
Whatever weather, cold or warm
Under the sky sipping blues
I shoot for the moon and end up a star.

Star shine keeps gazing at me, I am spit firing.
Money never been a concern
I let it rain on a girl while she rubs off me
I feel that ecstasy kicking in when you make that body sing

I can feel the heat, I can feel the wetness
My tongue touches the right spot
Stroke it up and down,
Slide in and you belong to me

Like magic, you trick my heart into falling
I got shawties' coming the right way
A freak in my bed, another in the couch
But you're my favourite kind of night

I like the way you lick me dry like you got O.C.D
One to the next, pour me a double on the rocks
Powder room with white stripes
Blame it on my A.D.H.D

I am not good nor I am bad, I am just wired perfectly flawed
She can feel her knees while I blow THC
I like the way you sin for me
Forget me and I will be right there to remind you again.

She

Falling like the autumn leaves...
Into the cold breeze she fades...
praying for a miracle.
Trying to find her way back home.

Knowing the pain of surviving a thousand little deaths.
Each dawn through the darkest night.
Shedding away the past, one more time...
Letting go of the trauma that made her.

Blossoming like a wildflower in a world of black and white roses...
She never let her emotions define who she is,
Rising every day from the dirt she plunged...
Finding a new hope from within.

Clouded thoughts of giving life up...
Thrust into the depths of her veins...
Confused with paranoia,
Deluded with the illusion of a perfect life.

She hides her pain in a smile...
A smile so contagious, making you awe.
You think that you know her...
But she is the wild one that can't never be tamed.

All she knows is to love again.
Even with her shattered heart broken into pieces...
Lost in between shadows,
But she won't let it turn her soul to darkness.

Shameless

Where did I go wrong with you??
How much liquor do you consume, she asked.
I said a lot, usually till I fall asleep.
She said it's not the alcohol, it's you.

All that love and still misbehaving,
Feel like you're just going to be keeping your heart safe.
All that flesh and nothing to lose...
Terrible, I felt, when you thought you're just being used for my pleasures.

I want to fall with you in your dream.
Wake up next to you to the morning glory.
In my heart I want,
But it's a past I like to live in, forgotten.

Where happiness was real...
With you, I like to live a story untold.
A touch can set you free...
Like freedom for the birds from a broken cage.

If I could I would, a lie I stumbled.
Not to fall for you again,
Complacent but acquainted!
Still trying to love you crazy.

Scared, you just leave, scared to love again.
Love is pain but you took my hand when the world seemed strange.
All of me for you, a smile is all that takes for me to fall for you again.
Still, I am shameless, to fall for you again.

I too have loved.

I can't go on without your breath this long.

It's like there's a part of me that feels incomplete when you are gone...

The more I try to fight it, the more I drown.

Rope me out one more time, don't let me be obscure.

I apologize for all the filth that you take me for,

Stranded in my own chaos-

I think I lost the only piece that held the puzzle together.

Now my madness is the only emotion I let myself embrace.

In these sheets I lay still

On these walls we wrote our love

The sensation of the touch, the lust!

Where once I made you skip your heartbeat

Bringing colour to my black and white life

A rush I cannot explain nor say but only crave.

You brought meaning to life instead of a moment bliss.

Was it the warmth of your ample bosom?

Now that you're gone like the wind,

Let me wash my soul again with sin,

A place to rest my head in peace,

Knowing that I too have loved a woman once.

I am the fallen one, to this angel.

Lost in the symphony of your notes,
 Melodious waves rush me,
You're the ecstasy in my blood,
That I keep coming back for more.

I am craving on a bed of white rocks,
Am I good or a good addict?
Cause all seems a bliss.
When I am held closely within your arms.

Thirsty lips, marooned heart
Two souls in a pot,
Simmering away in a flame!
A hope always remains.

They say time stops when you truly find love.
A while ago till the moment I met you,
I was drifting through the shallows,
To find myself mesmerized in a kiss-

Better than the always love you's.

Every morning my eyes meet you for the first time again,

And there is a spring in my feet.

You're the beat of my heart,

Falling for you all over again.

Everything changed but am I still the name?

Angelic and pure, you make me whole.

Like the star of the morning

I am the fallen one, to this angel.

Broken arrows.

You shattered my heart into a million pieces.

My dreams keep getting broken...

I can't seem to breathe.

So, I took a piece of my heart and cut my wrist to see how much I bleed.

I don't know if I will ever be the same.

They say time will heal...

Here I wait,

Living life by the minutes borrowed.

How can love be my pain?

In my arms, you were beautiful...

Now we don't even recognise who we are.

The butterflies have shed their wings.

The angels and the cupid had fallen,

God whispered when one door closes another open,

But I can't seem to find the right path.

Going round and round in this maze.

The murky clouds follow me around.
Making my eyes wet but no one seems to notice...
I am sad, sadder at night because you aren't beside...
Still, I hope the stars will align.

Aren't we all a projection of our own perception?
But I am still blinded by your reflection.
And you are still hiding behind love thinking about us.
Back in a day when we used to hold hands.

Angel wings.

I want you to kill me softly...
Love me like I am somebody...
Shoot me or blow me,
I want you to hit me hard.

Take me for the sin I am.
Tame me for the wild that I be.
Insane, eccentric and strange,
Show me how to be free.

Drench in my animosity...
I am careless who sees.
Disco lights and blues,
I am lost in your perfume.

My mind wants more but my body can't handle no more...
I want to stay awake but my eyes are blinded...
Rush me high, down me gentle,
Rock me to infinity.

Kiss me and lay me down...
Take my hand and hold me close...
Feel my heartbeat raising,
While I slip into OD.

Burning at both ends with desires,
The world keeps spinning.
But time seems to stop when you're with me,
And I lay here waiting for my angel wings.

Loving to a fault

Like a dream you came into my world
Felt like I was caught between heaven and what's divine.
Love never felt so blessed.
Dancing with you in my arms

The stars seem to shine brighter with you beside.
The breeze was cooler with my hands around your waist.
The moon and the stars smiled
The grass was greener on this side
The song of the birds was happier
Mornings sweet and harmonious
Each day better than the one before

Waking up to the melody of your breath
Soul to soul we touched,
Body to body we kissed,
Word to word we promised,
Grow old with me like a lullaby!

You found me when I was lost,
Took my heart under your wings,
Loved me like I am somebody,
Reconciled me back to life,

I loved you and you loved me,
The way we wanted each other kept us living.
Magical and beautiful.
Loving to a fault.

Magnetic persona.

I saw the fire in your eyes the day I caught you in my sight.
Tempting me every time I catch you in your lust.
You want to take the edge off and live your life.
You don't seem to care who sees and I don't mind...

She always lit the skies with her flames.
Rising brighter than the stars
Into the night she fades
Dancing away her pain.

She is the spark in everyone's heart,
The rush that gets you wishing for more...
She won't stay for none.
Babe is the dream that you wake up to...

She let it hail on a man like ice,
Make you feel cold and warm at the same time.
She'll make your darkest desires come alive,
Making you come back into her arms.

She moves to the rhythm of the beat,
Her ways get you feeling ecstatic,
Sexing you in ways so priceless.
Lost between her body's heat and perfume,

She got me fixated on love with her charm.
She tells me love is blind, so open your eyes,
I can't let you go like you can't get over me,
You got me attracted to your magnetic persona.

Strangers in a bed

Hold me through the night and let me wrong you till dawn,
Stay with me till the morning dew drops,
Lie to me that you love me to my eyes,
Even though we are just strangers in a bed.

She knows how to make a man feel alive,
She will make you young at heart,
Reminding you there's more to life than sex
Making you feel otherwise.

I can't help it, nor I can't resist.
There's no fighting this feeling when she is on top,
Like waves, she roughed me up.
Dominating my darkest desires

For her love comes with a price
Tears behind the smile, she confides,
Behind closed doors, she undresses her pain,
But she won't let it consume her shattered soul.

I need you to seduce me,

I need you to overwhelm me,

Like poison in my veins, take control of my bleeding heart,

I need you to be the death of my memories,

I don't know you, but I want you,

You don't want too but you won't hesitate.

But I'mma love you tonight like a drug,

Release me off my desperate itch.

The best feeling than a high.

Your eyes symphonies a thousand melodious notes my heart desires
You make me smile from my frown,
I don't know the answers yet,
But with you it feels right.

They say in time we get to love each other more,
It can be true cause every day I keep loving you more,
More than a touch, but as vibes twined.
Kiss me till I am sober

Material world didn't come as a cause,
Seasons didn't matter when we are under the sheets,
Didn't bother about others perception.
As long as I am with you and you're with me

Growing old never felt more alive.
I need you to be a part of my life,
Soul to soul you captured.
As you have sparked a fire inside

All of my life I was searching for a meaning, lost how to channel my thoughts.

Believing karma is a bitch with all that I have done,

But that changed with you,

Living in a world where you know you will be caught when you fall,

Loving a world with you beside

Actually, caring with no melodrama

It's the best feeling than a high.

Years in those eyes

Saw her on a moonlit night,
Lips red and hair down
Relaxed and laid back,
She said Hi and I said Hey,

Pass the joint she said,
I lit the torch and gave her,
Shook I sat as I saw another shot, she took
Puff! Puff! pass she smiled and passed,

Drunk out of my mind I kept talking,
Hypnotized by her eyes,
So beautiful, I felt alive.
I have never met someone so bewitching.

You can be with anyone but my heart can only be with you...
I fooled but felt the same
A love smiling from above,
A breeze in my heart

Sweet years in those mesmerizing eyes and blessings
Days pass but the cupid's arrows still sharp
First dance, first touch
First hug, first truth

As we both reminisce
A spark that never fades still keeps us warm.
Never photographed but memories keep us alive.
A hope from the Jewish carpenter still bonds us.

Wildfire.

I like the way it hurts
I like the way she taunts
Her flaws and imperfections.
She got me swirled in emotions,

Sweat dripping down her spine
Bewitched in the heat between her thighs
Each touch cold as ice
An insatiable pleasure every time.

Bruised knees and nights of blues
Feeling alive in our luscious lust
Moving slow in this fast life
Marooned with the fetish.

She is the thunderstorm I am struck with
She is the Illuminati to my darkness
A thousand pillows I have laid my head down on,
But with you each time it's exquisite.

She wants my affection

I am desensitized

Feeling not quite myself nor will I be someone else,

You're the wildfire, in which I want to wash away my sins.

Whispers of love

Like dew drops on a bloomed flower, you quench my thirst for love.

As the first kiss of the sun touches the green pastures, you're my ray of sunshine.

Air filled with romance and serenity,

Cupid had struck my heart silently.

Since my eyes gazed upon you,

My heart felt for you instantly.

I know it's an old cliche saying I fell for you the first time I ever saw you,

And there's a happily ever after like in the fairy tales,

But it's true with you, my love.

Lost in your mesmerizing eyes, the sun kissed lips and those cherry blossom cheeks.

You took my hand when the world seemed strange.

You got a light inside you that brightens my darkness.

You make me want to be the best version of myself.

Like beauty is in the eye of the beholder,
I can't help but fall for you each time I see you,
Once again, I want you like you want me too.

Like a kite dancing in a storm,
I find myself lost in your beauty and grace hoping the wind doesn't blow the lights out.
You make me see me for who I am.
Showering me with unadulterated and unconditional love.
Words can't describe someone who is as beautiful as you,
sweet like cinnamon and hotter than the brightest star.

Love never felt so good.
As far as the East is from the West,
My love for you never dies, you are right there to remind me again of what it is like to be loved,

Whispering in my ears I love you.
They say love is pain but with you I am willing to confide in.
Hold me close without hurting me,
I don't want this feeling to ever end.

My forbidden fruit

In darkness and cold, I was born,
The spark to survive kept me warm,
Hands plunged depth in dirt,
Heart numb, and hands rough-

Raised by my own will,
I have reached the top of the hill.
I look around and see my past bridging the future,
Left with enough love to be the hero of my own story,

Swept between my perception and reality,
Life teases her fantasies,
Love can be a beautiful burden.
Nothing compares to the high when I am in you.

Dried eyes and a fake smile,
Hefty pockets and loose fingers,
Hiding behind the person in the mirror,
To blend into societies melodrama,

Lost only to be found in your arms.
Sold my soul to be whole,
Everything seems to be grey,
But colourful in the eyes of the world.

Wicked dreams wake me up,
What do I chase now, I surrender,
The only wealth I can take with me is your forgiveness,
My forbidden fruit.

Pen pal.

Found her through the ink,
Sleepless nights and daydreams.
She is from the hills and I from the Ocean shores.
Never seen but our hearts spoke.

Like a ripple in the streams,
She and I whirled about our dreams,
Our friendship grew with roar,
But still never had seen.

She and I wrote with passion,
Sowing our compassion,
Between us, there was no deception,
Still our eyes did not meet.

There were depths in words,
Through melodious poems and prose,
We inked our hearts,
But not a silent word was spoke.

As true as seasons change,
Our friendship was meticulous but strange.
Into the wind I was blown away, like a paper plane,
In our hearts we remain, my pen pal.

Kill me softly!

Am I pushing my luck with you?
Am I being dishonest to my heart?
Cause I feel like there's no happy ending between us.
All I keep feeling now is you falling apart and apart.

Drowning in a pool of dreams,
I keep suffocating in my own thoughts,
I look up and all I see is your face,
So let me breathe in your love.

You rocked me like molly,
You were the ecstasy to my euphoria.
It would be a lie if we say we didn't feel a thing,
You were the rush in my veins.

All I can do is still love hard even though the pain stings,
But love is supposed to be sweet like a melody that gets us dreaming
A connection between two souls
Like a fire burning brightly.

Isn't love a fantasy of seek and find?
I found you when you were searching for me
We thought the world of each other
You are my light; I should've seen it in your eyes.

At the beginning of the end
If you're going to break my heart,
Then kill me softly!
Cause then I could be with you a little while longer.

Sad girls and bad boys.

Sad girls and bad boys
Cold enough for the heart to freeze
Feelings of misbehaving,
Only to find yourself lost in falling.

There's no place to hide from the tears
Desperate to see if happiness exists
Another beautiful day,
Washed away in the sea of dreams.

Through the blackest day and darkest night
Life got in the way but where?
The lights are dimming,
 How can I hold you when I don't even have myself.

I shoot my veins and get lost in the trance
An escape from my immoral thoughts.
Molly and L.S.D rush me high
But it is always you that I need when I am coming down.

Bitter birthdays and Christmas.
Contemplating the self in the mirror
Selfish to give love away as you love me
Buried with the past burden and broken hopes

It's sad but I do you wrong
It's bad but I want to do more
We don't get older together
But the sun still sets.

Rose tinted eyes.

Should I go?
Should I leave?
Tell me do you still feel?
Tell me you still believe?

You love the way I look at you.
You crave the way I touch you.
The more you're apart,
The more I am deep in you.

Leaping towards the deserted ways.
Into the depths we instigate.
Paranoid and ignorant.
Only to find lost in each other's arms.

The walls are building itself.
Confusing what is real.
Somewhere we still hope.
Searching for the better half.

The pain we feel will heal.
For a better tomorrow we endure.
Nothing seems to be but you.
Seeing us through rose tinted eyes.

Used to use you.

Fingers crossed deep in you,

Baby I let you use me.

She screams my name,

She says control my heart cause the feelings aren't mutual.

I find solace when I am inside her,

Here with me, I want you to be you.

Take what's left of my soul,

Drain me from my sin.

I hold you up, you bring me down like downers,

One step away from you to find myself engulfed by you again,

But the pictures still fall on me.

Should I or could you please shut my mind?

Unbuttoned and free

I feel the blood rush when you go downtown.

Even though I stand high than you, I feel so small.

But you seem to reach fine when you take me by the lips,

I ask too much and show too little,

You don't seem to bother,

Says life is like butter,

Melts when hot and takes shape when chilled.

I used to use you like you used me, but sex kept us together.

We followed our hearts, and the stars showed our colour.

In separate ways but never apart than a dollar bill,

Meticulous to a point of melancholy.

When forever isn't long enough.

You make me feel happy and beautiful
You make me feel whole again,
Made those thoughts of despair disappear,
Hold me tightly and never let go.

You took my hand when the world seemed strange,
My flaws were just perfect for you,
Cash less, no suit and tie still I was a man in your eyes,
You made me feel like I was somebody.

Drunk, high and with a smile,
Dance with me and don't let go.
My heart beats with the rhythm of your heart
Your love is all I need.

You took my shattered dreams and mend,
Appreciated me for the sin that I am,
Took my perception and made it something wonderful,
And you did it again and again like it's the first time.

All over again in your lap I lay my head,
Each stroke on my head gives me a new butterfly,
We made love looking at the stars,
Finding solace in our faults.

You made the choice as I have chosen you,
We found that piece that holds us,
Lost and found in cupid's breath,
Baby, when forever isn't long enough.

Mysterious ways

Say I never let you go,
Say I want to hold you close.
Together we can love.
Start as you mean to go.

Faith got me high!
Hope got us into believing again,
Is it heaven because I see you now?
Take me all away.
Soul to soul so close,

A spark to pyre,
Untamed and raw,
Pure as snow.
Bewitched between thoughts,

A fleeting glimpse of rays,
The sparkling in our eyes,
Fading like shadows into the night!
As apples of gold in pictures of silver,
You and I defined each other.

Making way to the path beyond,
Praying for things to go smooth,
The sensation of touch,
Emotions and lust!

Pleasures that we thought never existed,
Heart to heart we never faded,
Engulfed in each other's desires,
Lost in the stars shooting in the sky above us,
Apart yet, we see,
Finding oneself in mysterious ways.

With you, my world revolves.

The more you want me,
The less I want you,
And the more I need you,
You keep fading away.

The love that I give you,
The rose petal kisses you give away.
But at least we both are beautiful,
Endorsed in complacent.

In an abyss able to find flashes of hope!
Her heart only knows bliss.
A kiss makes your sorrows shallow...
Shining a vivid light to the darkness.

The less I knew you, the more I adored you...
The more I know you, the harder it is to forget.
Far as seasons change and the seven seas wind!
Emotion is all we feel, a shoulder beside.

Lost in your breath!
You made me skip a heartbeat.
Ever holding you close to the chest...
With you my world revolves around.

Presence of you.

Listen baby don't disturb me,
When I am smoking my herb...
Baby just be free,
Together we can smoke in peace.

Happy and glee,
No strain, no tension,
No fuzz, no lies...
Believe and pass the torch.

Satisfying my soul...
I smoke Ganja when it's raining,
I smoke Ganja when the sun shines...
When you feel the breeze, you feel the magic.

No sticks and seeds, only greens!
Chill in a chillum, bong or pass the joint,
I love you, Mary Jane!
Lucy and Mandy on the stand.

Meditated to the vibe...
Heart beating to the rhythm...
Let it be indica or sativa,
I am blown in the presence of you.

Knocking at your door

Met you on a summer night...
Now I am talking to myself
I am losing my mind when you aren't beside
A tale, I can't help write!

Scared what should I expect or meet?
Love isn't my forte so I can't follow
As our breath lifted away ego
I am rooted, so I can't let go...

You're the queen of my heart
The soul of my life
The lust to my whispers
The sorry estranging my pain

I keep finding myself through you
a euphoria, I can't get enough
Is it love or am I believing! dreaming?
if so, I don't want to wake up from this multiverse

Cause I want you up a kiss close always

Your touch sends a rhythm down my spine

My tongue touches the right spot

Fingers curled and sheets tight

Be the mother of my child

The epiphany to my throne

You're not a drug but you're the only one that can give me this high

Be my best friend, be my shoulder besides,

You got me knocking at your door, cause with you, the world seems fine.

An ode to love

I am trying to get lost in that love...
A feeling that quilts my heart...
I want to get found in your world...
As you have opened my eyes in your shine.

What have you done to me...
Cause I am feeling a rush...
From tip to toe to down my spine...
You're the nectar to the butterflies you put inside mine.

With you I am lost in the melody...
The first we met eyes, time stopped for me...
You're the song that gets me dreaming...
You're the wisdom to my being.

I love you so hard, it hurt...
Never close my eyes, so I wouldn't miss...
Hang on to me and don't let go...
I find myself entangled, clueless where to start.

My life graced like the summer breeze...

Falling for you each time I see you, once again...

A feeling quite known yet unknown...

With the stars above as our witness, come to me.

A million to one shot.

Did the fire we initially have disappear?
Did the spark turn the amber into ashes-
Igniting out the pyre...
Did the flames turn against us?

How much we have become!
To a hope that see the light.
Emotions left scattered,
A bond we unite.

Nights in despair...
Days Motionless and sigh,
Dates keep passing...
Letting fate, faith it out.

Painting sunshine to my darkness...
Woman you swept me off my feet!
Bringing colours in to the void,
Of glee and passionate impish.

Still on the shore, waiting for you...
On the other side she awaits...
Drowning in the love,
A million to one shot.

Ghosts of the past

Tonight, I let go of my dreams
Those sleepless nights, I lay rest
Make peace with myself
My wandering feelings ceases my thoughts

Enticing as it may
Harmonious as it maybe
Saccharine as a melody
With patience, this too shall pass

The time we had, I would always cherish
You were more than a heart
In a crowded world,
You showed me that I am not alone

As there is a beautiful beginning
I suppose there is always a bittersweet end
All we can do is love in between,
And rejoice to the angel's chime

Indulging in our guilty pleasures
We forgot the future and the past
Living life to the high at that moment
Never needed more, never needed less

But as all good things come to an end,
Love took the toll on me again
Now I am in my rocking chair,
Reminiscing about my ghosts of the past.

Yet her

She headed towards the sun
Her flame lit the sun up
Love took her soul
The fire slaved itself to her

Yet her.

The stars and the moon gazed
The ocean roared, the streams overflowed
Thunderstruck, an empty life
A hope, a hand took her...

Yet her.

Half-life worked in wage
Yet another, she hopes will be bliss
Death around the corner
Is that the end, or my life often

Yet her.

Different pillows, different scented candles
Four walls, different towels
Can't seem to feel the face
A pleasure to ease the past

Yet her.

Twisted maybe, but yet she wants it
Prayers forever answered her mind whispers
Still, she hopes for a touch
A release from her introspective self

Yet her.

Bodies together in a muddle of money
A paradise she lives now
And she asks, am I enough
For a thought of a wedding ring

Yet her.

False hopes

And I thought she would never leave
Forever stay, forever never fade
Here with me, beside me
Telling me everything will be alright

Bold yet so enchanting
Sorrowful, disguised under a smile
Beautiful as the sunrise
You keep getting lost in her mesmerizing eyes

Young and rich in heart
Shining brighter than the horizons hue
She'll make you feel warm like a mother's touch
Alluring you into her arms

Hope can be deceitful
Love can be pain
But without sadness, one can never truly understand what happiness means
Like a cocktail of feelings

As a song you keep playing in my mind

You were the rhythm to my heartbeat

Thought it was you and I till the end of time

As a lullaby that never grows old

You never broke my heart; you still keep it from harm

All we can do is keep treasuring the memories day after day

Reminiscing to move forward

Cause we surrendered to each other without giving false hopes.

Everything love and other intoxicants

Frozen in sadness but with you I am lost in the symphony,

A try to escape the actuality.

I feel the blood rush and it's amazing,

I need you to take me by the lips.

Waking up to the bliss of the stardust you shower,

Existing somewhere between dream and reality,

What a beautiful place to be,

Never facing the crash of losing you.

You rock my world like molly,

Arouse me like cocaine and down me like codeine,

Puff puff pass that o.g, never afraid to o.d,

Lay me in your arms and sing me a lullaby.

She wants my affection,
I am desensitized but with you I feel invincible,
I keep confiding in her like she is my shrink,
When all she wants is me to seduce her blindly.
Lost in your beauty,
All I can keep thinking of is you out loud,
Fleeting glimpses of sweet memories.
I will do it all over again with you.

Happiness is a state of mind,
Heaven is a place with you,
Paused back and forth but never separated,
From everything love and other intoxicants.

Au revoir my love.

Rain drops falling from heaven...
In the distance I see your face...
The mist keeps shadowing my eyes...
But in my heart, I feel your warmth.

Like calm waters before rage...
With you I feel complete...
I realize this feeling is true...
Without you my world will be desolate.

In your eyes I find myself lost...
In your love I find myself saved...
The morning to my star...
Keep me in your prayers.

Cupid had struck my heart.
The tension between us makes me aroused...
Wild, passionate and serene...
Au revoir my love.

Forever Bloom.

Look at them they said
Don't look at them some
They are the bad choices they uttered
Who drinks and smoke ganja they spread...

We are the somebody's
Raised In a world of dreams and fantasies
We marched from the bottom we call home
We don't give a flying fuck to the moon
Now or then

Like a halo, they surround me in their bliss
The breeze just feels right with us together
Everything just seems manageable with unity and love
From dusk till our dawn

Moving on, one step. In the moment
Memories shoot like crystals in a snort
Still the endless cheers carry on
Like wine, we aged good

Some call them friends, some brothers and some sisters

When the time you realize that bond is something more than you

Everything just seems right like two bongs back-to-back

Me and my soul crew on cloud 9

Shout out to us because we are the best

Still balling the game like a player

Still tipping, still tripping balls

But always there for each other's minutes...

Me and my friends, forever bloom.

My immoral whispers.

I am no demon, I am the almighty,
I am the alpha and the Omega,
I am the emperor, I am the fallen,
I am the king; I am the Kong.

Lost souls allied side…
I got God with me.
I am the devil you see,
Heaven, hell and in between.

From the depths of the inferno…
To the shores of the pearly gates…
Cast out to where death awaits…
Torn between shadows.

I got all that I need…
I got all of me…
I want it all to my greed…
My pride and ego.

Holy or unholy,

Ethical or cynical,

Finding love in hate,

Listening to my immoral whispers.

Pixie dust

Season's change but time stops for me when I am laying my head on your lap...

Kisses soft as rose petals on my lips...

The touch of your ample bosom on my body, holding me tightly...

The world seems to be glittering with pixie dust...

A sense of glee fulfils my heart...

With you I am never lost...

My love for you runs in infinite...

But I keep getting lost for words to express how unconditionally beautiful you are to me.

Our love is fun but never a game...

Our love is pure but never we let it be toxic...

Our love is blind but we see each other as who we are...

Our love is true but never in vain.

Never cared for what others think...
We let our lives speak for themselves...
I felt for you and you caught me with open arms...
We got that burning desire for each other.

All that matters to me is what you think...
What I ever want is for you to be whole with me...
You never let me be someone I am not...
Is this what true love really means??

Now I feel like I am after all blessed...
My perspective of this world had changed...
A past where something was missing and now, I know what...
Since that beautiful day I laid my eyes on you.

Rolling stone.

Baby I am sorry if I made you think I don't need you...
Baby I am sorry if I made you think I don't love you...
Baby I am sorry if I made you think that we don't believe now...
Baby I am sorry if we paused.

It's bittersweet because I need you more than ever,
And I don't want us to fight, never
Cause I don't want us to hate...
Cause you're the fire to my warmth.

Sinned in the love that you give,
Wash me in the blessings that you shower...
I want to kiss you like a lover...
You're the light in my universe.

I am thinking what to say cause baby you're just the type...
Time to kiss the tears goodnight...
Wake up to your sunshine...
Gaze upon your bewitching eyes, my starshine.

I got these feelings for you,
And only you can help me through...
Tell me how...
You got my heart bleeding for you.

It will be a lie if I say I don't need you...
I don't say goodbye anymore,
I am a rolling stone...
And baby you're my rock.

My solace

I am not trying to hit on somebody...
Cause my heart has already crashed on you...
Sunken in dreams in an ocean of symphony...
Take my hand and don't let me drown.

Whisper in my ears those magic words...
Awake me from my estranged sleep,
Don't let me drift away like dead wood...
Kiss me to life from my desolate past.

Away and a step behind but not lost...
So close but yet so distant...
Miles apart from your cherry red lips,
But I don't mind as long as our hearts beat at the same rhythm.

Come to me on my low...
Take my blackened soul and shine a ray of hope!
Cleanse me from the dirt that I have become...
Show me the light on the other side.

I need you to scream my name...
I need you to screech the demon out of me...
Restless to the nerves, I suffer...
I need you to be my solace.

Flesh to flesh, tears and sweat...
Love can be painful but divine at the same time...
I want to end the dusk with you in my arms...
And wake the dawn with your hand on my palms.

Screw me holier.

Let's smoke, drink and dance,
Eat, talk and laugh.
69 and wine would be nice!
Waking up to each other's arms in a bed of rose petals seems divine.

Is this love at first sight?
A fling or something over with a caramel flan?
All I can say is my tooth is sweet for you,
A sugar rush from tip to toe.

Up she goes, down she wiggles,
Up mines and don't fidget,
Making us piping hot under the weather,
Sweat, spit and thunder.

Smack that, bounce that,
Kiss her, lick her,
Tease her, touch her,
Caress, smother and taunt.

As her fingers crawl deep in,

And her moans echo,

Wetter and moist as the angels' cry-

My tongue dancing between her thighs.

Freed in with our lust,

Sins forgotten and desires reignite,

Tomorrow is a new horizon,

But tonight! All we could say aloud is screw me holier.

Shooting star

Through heaven and hell, we walked...
I showed you the pearly gates,
And lured you into the devil's den...
From the final chapter we shall start.

The devil took advantage of her soul,
Showed no mercy at all...
She felt for his charm...
From ashes to dust she faded...

From human to demon, she changed!
No love, just lust thy begin.
No one cared like tears in the rain...
Sweat, blood and pain.

The devil is keen with his words...
Possessed her back and forth.
Everything that has a beginning as an end!
Amour not to be seen, still passion sowed.

Now the devil has changed to humanity...

She wouldn't believe for his crave...

Like flesh to earth from grave...

Devil may cry, but in her heart, he remains like a shooting star.

Without rose tinted glasses.

I cannot fight this feeling and look the other way
Girl, I want you even if you don't reciprocate
Stay with me as I want to be with you
Love me like I love you under my sheets...

I love the way you touch me
I know the way you want me in you
I like the way you mourn my name out loud
Take me by the tongue and I know you...

You're the addiction for my craving
The rush I try to flush out
A numbness throughout my veins
But I can't help it, I want more

You always shut down when it comes to love
Scared to fall for again
You don't ever have to rush, let's take it step by step
A simple touch can set your heart on fire

I will care for you because you're worth it
I like the way u work it
Tempting me every time I catch u in your lie
I know you want me like I want you…

Awakening next to you is the thought that wakes me
Morning's sweet like cinnamon and nights of blues
I like that we don't ever have to pretend and wonder
I want you for who you are like the way you see me, without rose tinted glasses…

With You

Baby you got me thinking of you

You got me feeling butterflies

You got me attracted to your fiery persona

You got me loving so hard.

I love the way you dance

I love the way you look with your god graced smile

I love everything about you and more

Your eyes are so gorgeous like the sun rose in those.

You and I are from different worlds

You and I are like wine and water

You and I might be strange for each other

But it's only you that I want forever.

I promise it's going to be alright

Ain't too much I can do, but what I do I would from all my heart

A bit of love can change the world we see

We are who we choose to be, ourselves.

Oh! I want to dance with you under the stars

Oh! I want to talk with you till the dusk kiss goodbye

Oh! I want to hold you in my arms and paint the skies with our dreams

Oh! I want to sing and scream with you on a mountain.

Into the night, I want to fade away with you

To a morning so beautiful but not as beautiful as you

Heaven is where I am with you

So please take my hand and don't let go.

My silver lining on cloud nine.

Babe if you got a heart to borrow
Please take my love than sorrow
Lost in your breath, I am hollow
You make me feel so mellow...

Our love is like fine wine, getting mature with time
My world keeps spinning with you in my arm
Joyous and amorous, so flaw some
You make me feel naked and beautiful

Seeing you in black and white eyes,
Baby you bring out the colours alive...
My skies filled with rainbows and unicorns now
With you, it's magical like our story's a fairy tale.

Your lips so supple, your eyes keep talking
Silky hair falling on sides, so lushing
Red cheeks keep blushing like the sunrise
Shining like the sunshine, you brighten my day every day.

From dusk till dawn, she never makes me feel alone

Like a bloomed wildflower, she is the nectar in my veins

Sweet like honey with a tinge of cinnamon

She completes me...

She was the missing piece of my puzzled life

You're the choice I made like I am the one who you chose

Both of us felt right for each other

You are my silver lining on cloud nine.

Surrealistic love

I can't figure you out fully
But I want you to fulfil me
Take me by the hand and be honest with me
You want me like the way I want you madly…

I am drunk, I am high, I got poker chips
Chip on my shoulder
Never afraid to unlock hearts
But it's with you I feel that euphoria

I give it to you just the way you like it
You always turn me on the way I fantasize
Tongue locked and lost in your breath
I like the way you mourn my name softly…

Intoxicated in love
Hundreds goes pass in fleeting glimpse
But you're the one that made me skip a heartbeat
Making everything seem almost surreal…

Living in darkness is no longer an option
Ever since I have been graced by the light in you
Shining like the sun, so divine
You're the sunshine in my pocket...

We found each other on a simple day
A day that I hold dear to my chest
Around you I feel like I am floating on clouds
A kiss to remind us, you belong to me and I belong to you.

Under these quilts

Gazing at each other's eyes till the stars fade
Talking till the dawn shines its rays
Holding hands throughout the night
I just want to love you tonight and ever.

Faithful forever being with you
You make my day good enough for a smile
Stay with me for now and be with me still
You are the centre of my dreamy world.

Like the touch of a dew drop on the skin on a chilly morning
The touch of your cherry lips on mine
Shook me from my tip to toe
A transcendental opulence...

Life seems to move fast when I am with you
Time seems to get lost when you're on top of me
A minute with you is a like a lifetime of happiness I cherish
But twenty-four hours just isn't cutting it.

I want to grow old with you as partners

Be my crime, be my sin

The only thing that I pray now is to give you all that I dream

When you keep saying it's just me all you want...

Sex Stories, different chapters

Summer breeze to cool us off

I want you and you want me, we are happy

While we make love under these quilts.

You're my missing puzzle pieces.

I see fire in your eyes when I look at you...

A shockwave running through my veins when I touch you...

You don't ever have to try, your exquisite the way you are...

I want to do this dance with you.

Since I met you, my night turned white...

But my heart's still black and cold, a past I've come to pass...

When I am with you, I seem to forget my tears.

I am just trying to keep my love alive.

Is this what heaven feels like?

I have been on the road for so long to know...

New and strange, yet so graced.

I want you but why do I feel pigeon holed?
Obsessed to an extent of resentment...
Still can't keep the hands of each other,
You got that feeling that pulls me back every time.
Sex, narcotics and us, we are wonderful the way we are.

It's a crazy beautiful world, when I am in it with you...
Time seems to wander when we are lost together...
Everything I need, now I have but I want more,
I am a fiend and you're the angel I need.

More than friends but less than lovers...
I feel naked and complacent...
We take each other for who we are...
You're my missing puzzle pieces.

Let me be your last mistake

She came to me like a cold mist
Clouding my reality
Making my heart yearn for warmth
The touch that chilled my bones

Like a leap of faith, I surrender to this sweet suffer
A long way from where she kissed me
Still gunning for you, I shot
But lost somewhere in the distance

The fire has calmed its rage
Leaving it's burnt bruises
But love somehow kept its spark
Smothering behind the shadowing smoke

As a cocktail of drugs couldn't do
How much ever material couldn't buy
Nothing can sweep me anymore
Since I tasted you

A past I wish in present to be my future
Waiting desperately for an answer
Sleepless nights and daydreams
An irresistible itch I can't resist

Wedding bells ring at her door
A step closer to our chapter being closed
On my knees I shout
Let me be your last mistake.

Schizophrenic

We were broken long before hopes
Still am I unforgiven?
God save my soul,
I don't want to end up a slave to myself.

Adapt, adoptee to feelings unknown
Same head, different persons
The endless whispers
Somewhere torn between dreams and reality.

Shunned Strangers and close ones
Mind concealed between the four walls
Fidgeting thoughts play in the background
To somehow find a way to get lost in tranquility.

Finding hope in fear when things seem daunting
Drugs sometimes feels like the only remedy
Overdosing till the brain freezes numb,
An escape from the endless thinking.

False perception and hallucinations
A withdrawal from personal relation
A sense of mental fragmentation
Confused between fantasy and delusion.

Lacking purpose and conviction
Like the person you were died, yet still living
The boundaries set looks different
Still breathing, a minute in a day of a schizophrenic.

Queen of Misery

And there she is in her world…
Magic and the breeze from a thousand wings.
In her zone, on her throne…
She radiates like the horizon hue.

Bringing colours to the void to whomsoever is graced by her…
A touch can leave you in the clouds…
Every time her hair tingles my face…
It's enough to know deep down that you are smitten.

She dances to her soul…
A rhythm you can't unhear!
A broken heart mended with her own will,
Still, she poured the chalice full with love.

Life never gave her lemons,
She worked a step up a day…
In a world where there's no hold bars,
A dragon by nature, she let her roar hear a thousand miles…

She doesn't wear a halo,

She doesn't care about your melodramas,

A woman that can free you from your inequity,

The one whom you fall for once.

Oh, my queen! that leaves me in misery when you're not beside.

So close but two worlds apart...

A bliss to be besotted with...

A love worth infinite rising moon.

My unseen friend named God.

If I am the devil,
What should I fear they ask?
I said I am afraid of the insecurity I get when I feel like you are not hearing my voice,
Where my answers stop...

They seem to see I am dry without love
They seem to wonder why I am so bizarre
But I guess I seem to get through each day
Tears shed, but still past shadows the bliss.

Time kept me but pressure mounds deep like a scar,
Cop cars, drugs, and rock,
But nothing else matters,
When angels kept falling like stardust.

In greed for a memory,
A vibe where we choose to be free,
Living day one a day a time,
Wasted to wake up from a dream.

The strange it becomes,

The stranger I am to you.

A step colder but a foot away from the rain,

To get lost in the warmth of your scent.

I am sorry, but I can't seem to conjure to your thoughts.

I am watched, but I seem to be alone.

Every day, I open my eyes

In a wish to have a glimpse of my unseen friend named, God.

www.ingramcontent.com/pod-product-compliance
Lightning Source LLC
LaVergne TN
LVHW061619070526
838199LV00078B/7339